KU-076-267

Contents

The Living Word

Eileen Caddy

FINDHORN
Press

Edited by Roy McVicar
Design and layout by Ronald Morton
Cover design by Thierry Bogliolo
Printed by WSOY, Finland

Published by
Findhorn Press
The Park, Findhorn
Forres IV36 0TZ
Scotland
tel +44 (0)1309 690582 / fax 690036
email books@findhorn.org
http://www.findhorn.org/findhornpress/

Foreword

The short prayers or meditations which are found
in this book were given to me at various times over
the years, and I would use them in the sanctuary
before a time of stillness or when in need.

They were given to me by the 'still small voice'
within, the voice I have heard and lived by for
many years. I call the voice 'God's voice'. You can
call it what you will.

I hope that they will be as helpful and uplifting
to you as they have been to me.

Eileen Caddy
Findhorn Foundation

Morning prayer

Here we are at the beginning of another day
We dedicate this day to You
We dedicate our thoughts and efforts
To the bringing forth of Your good.

You are our strength
Our life
Our guiding light
You are the power in us
That perfects everything that concerns us
You are the love in us
That harmonises every situation
That forgives every hurt.

All through this day
We will remember
That we live and move and have our being
In You.

We will entrust all our plans
Our hopes
And dreams to You
Knowing that in You
All things find their right fulfilment.

We are aware
Of Your loving presence throughout the day
And know that in that state of awareness of You
We are filled with love, strength, peace and joy.

We ask that You use us
As you will
To bring about Your wonders and glories.

Beginnings

I was shown a very busy highway with traffic moving to and fro at great speed. No one had any time to look at anything as they were so busy going places.

Then I was shown a country lane with the peace and beauty of the flowers in the hedgerows, the birds and the tiny animals moving in the undergrowth, and I felt and saw God in everything, and there was great peace and tranquillity in my heart.

I heard the words: 'Start each day in My peace and stillness. Then you can go forth and face whatever the day may bring in perfect peace and joy.

'Start today.'

The way you start each day is so important
Let there be a song of praise
And gratitude in your heart
An awareness of My limitless love and abundance
A knowing that there is time
To do everything that needs to be done.
It is up to you how you use that time.

Let Me guide you throughout the whole day
Place all in My hands:
Yourself
Your work
Your affairs
Your interests
Your activities
Let Me work in and through you.

Let go of any feeling of being tied to time
Flow with it
And you will be in the right place
At the right time
Doing the right thing.

Never put anything off because it seems difficult
Know that I will give you the energy and wisdom
To accomplish everything
In the right spirit
And with joy.

There is time for everything
When you are attuned to Me
Attune now.

What is your first thought on waking?

Is it one of pure joy for another wonderful day
Or do you dread what today may bring?

Is it an effort to get into tune
And into rhythm with this day?

Can you wake up with a song of praise
And thanksgiving in your heart?

What a difference it will make for you
When you can do this
When you can start the day
By putting on rose tinted spectacles
And seeing everything through them
Throughout the day.

See all the very best
All the positive.

This day
Can be the most wonderful inspiring day
But it is up to you what you do with it.

Why not start off
By giving thanks - to open your heart?
The more thankful you are
The more open you are
To all the wonderful things the day can bring.

Love
Praise
And gratitude
Fling open wide the portals
And allow the light to stream in
Revealing all the very best in life.

The moment you wake up
You can decide
What kind of day it is going to be for you.

Wake up with joy in your heart
A song of praise and thanksgiving on your lips
And know that I am with you
And all is very very well.

Let this be a day of days.

'Be ye transformed by the renewing of
  your minds.'

A snake cannot grow
Without shedding its old skin
A baby chick cannot emerge from its shell
Without cracking it open
A baby cannot be born
Without emerging from its mother's womb.

These are natural processes
Which have to come about to bring changes
Step by step they take place
And nothing can stop them.
If the baby chick does not have the strength
To break out of the shell
It will die.

There is a right time for everything.
You can try to prevent changes taking place
Because you feel safe and secure where you are
And would rather stay
In the confines of that which you know
Than move out into the unknown
But in those confines
You will suffocate
And die.

So change
Keep on changing
I am with you always.

All the time you are growing
And expanding in consciousness
You are beginning to understand
The mystery
The wonder of life eternal
And your realisation of oneness with Me
The creator of life
The creator of all.

Step by step
You move onward and upward
Filled with peace
Tranquillity
And serenity
Realising that all is in My hands
Therefore you have nothing to concern
yourselves with.

Become as little children
Free and joyous
And life will be a continual source of delight
    for you
A veritable wonderland
With something new and exciting
Round every corner.

You know by now
That when things begin to happen
They happen at great speed
And everything falls into place
Perfectly
But the timing has to be right.

When winter comes
And closes in on you
You feel it will never end
But before you realise what is happening
Spring almost unobtrusively starts to
    break through:
The daylight is longer
The life force is there all around you
Bursting through on every side.
Before you know it
Winter has gone
The glorious spring is with you in all its wonder.

This is what is happening with the New - now.
Like the spring it is here
The winter, the old, has passed away
But some of you have not fully realised
Or accepted it
Until you do so
Your eyes will not be open to the wonder of it all.

Think of the joy of the first snowdrops
    and crocuses
The first signs of spring
What a lot you would miss
If you did not appreciate these signs.

Open your eyes
Miss nothing that is taking place at this time
You may feel nothing is happening
But I tell you a tremendous amount is happening
And is poised there on the etheric
Simply waiting to be brought down
And manifested on the physical
For all to see.

Move into new realms
Break all old moulds
All that would restrict you
And hold up your growth
And expansion.

Infinite life
Cannot be constrained within a narrow concept
Infinite love
Cannot be confined in one relationship.

Open your heart wide
And love all humankind
All creation.

Move into those higher realms
Where all is one
And you know the meaning of no separation.

Let go the lesser
So that the greater may be free to manifest
Be aware of the expansion of growth
Within you.

Greet this day with joy
Put joy into each activity of this day
It is a new day
A glorious day
Blessed by Me.

Look not to the past
Nor to the future
But enjoy this day to the full
And flow with it.
Resist not change
Grow and unfold
Reveal those many hidden gifts and talents
    within you.

Hide not your light
Your love
Your joy
Let these many facets shine forth
And do your part
To help make this world a better place
To help bring heaven down on Earth.

Why not start doing it now?

Happiness is not something to get out
    of life
But a natural by-product of putting your best
    into life.

Close your eyes
And see clearly.
Cease to listen to the noise without
And you will hear truth
That still small voice within.

Be silent
And your heart will sing with joy.

See no separation
And you will find oneness.

Be gentle
And you will need no power.

Be patient
And you will achieve all things.

Let life unfold like a flower
Be ever aware of the divinity within
Know that all is well
And never fail to give thanks for everything
For gratitude keeps your heart open
And the love flowing.

Let My divine love flow through you
Out to all you are in contact with this day.
Be this now.

Let your heart and mind be stayed on Me.
Dwell on all the beauty and wonders in life.

Go about with your eyes wide open
And appreciate the beauty all around you.

Be not bowed down by self-concern
And so miss all the wonders in life.

Take one day at a time
And appreciate that day to the full.

Let every moment of it
Be filled with love and thanksgiving.

Give thanks for everything you have
For everything you receive
For everything you are going to receive.

Never cease to give thanks
For it is a positive attitude towards life
And the very act of giving thanks
Draws the very best to you.

It helps to keep your heart and mind open
It helps to keep your consciousness expanding.

You can always find something to give thanks for
And as you start to do this
And start to count your blessings
They will increase;
You then realise how mightily blessed you are
That you are indeed endowed with all this
    world's riches
For all your good and perfect gifts come from
God.

As you give
So do you receive
This is the law.

Rejoice and give eternal thanks
For you know that you live for ever
And you do it one day at a time
Living each moment fully and gloriously
Forgetting the past
With no concern for the future
Simply accepting that life has no beginning
And no end
That life is eternal
And you are hope eternal.

I am life
I am within you
I live and move and have My being in you.

I am infinite
You are one with Me
You are one with all life

Silence and Meditation

I was aware of a great noise all around
and then the noise died down and there was a
great stillness.

In the stillness I could hear what
seemed to be the faint ticking of a clock.
As I listened very intently the sound
became louder and clearer. I heard the words:
'I am always here. But unless you become
consciously aware of Me and of My divine
presence you cannot hear My voice. Therefore
still that which is without so that you can hear that
which is within.'

Take each day as it comes
Rededicate yourself to the service of
    all humankind.

In the stillness go deep within
Listen to that still small voice.

Seek not the answer from without
But ever from within
For all is within
All you need to know is right there inside.

In quietness enter the secret place
Within your being
There you are at peace
And listen.

You feel the warmth of love welling up in you
You hear the words 'love one another'.

Put first things first
Then all else will be added unto you.

In quietness and in confidence
Wait
Know that all is very very well
All is working out perfectly.

Meditate in stillness
And discover the power that is within

To meditate
Is to know the power of stillness

In many ways
Nature reveals the power of stillness:
The blooming of a flower is a quiet process
The miracle of dawn and the glorious sunrise
Is not heralded with any noise
The moon and stars appear without fanfare.

All creation
Is sustained
By silent
Imperceptible
Unfailing law.

Be still
And know
That the 'I am' within you
Is God.

Start this day in quiet meditation.
Relax all busy thoughts
Remove all barriers of doubt
Worry
Anxiety
That may block you from direct contact with Me.

Let Me work in and through you
And know that with Me all things are possible.

Let Me restore in you
Confidence
Faith
Belief
Courage.
Be afraid of nothing
Be fearless and undaunted.

Go into the silence
For it is in the silence things unfold
In the silence you reach the heights
In the silence you are reborn, renewed, revitalised.

Silence is golden
All things spring from divine silence.
In silence
Give thanks for everything
Count your many blessings
Be consciously aware of My limitless love
Of My limitless abundance.

In the stillness
We are aware of the beat of our hearts
It is life
Life more abundant.

Life is God
God is all -
All creation
The vastness of the universe
Yet the tiniest atom.

Life is in everything
For God is in everything
There is nothing God is not in.

As we expand our consciousness
We are aware of the oneness of all life
We are aware that we are that oneness.

Our hearts beat
In unison
With this oneness
Oneness
Oneness
Oneness.

Be conscious of our closeness
Be still and listen.

If you are constantly busy
Rushing around
You forget to listen
You wonder why things do not go smoothly
Why you are not at peace.

Put Me first in everything.
Time spent in the stillness
Is never a waste of time.

Attune to Me
The source of all creation
Let My creativity flow through you
And be you.

Wait upon Me
And renew your strength.

Every moment of waiting time
Can be spent with your mind stayed on Me
In close communion with Me.

Raise your consciousness
And instead of becoming frustrated
Because you have to wait for something
   or someone
Give thanks for that time
And use it productively
By turning to Me
Tuning to Me
Talking and listening to Me.

Relax in My love
And in turn pour forth that divine love
Out to the world.

Next time you find yourself waiting for someone
Or for something to happen
Think of these words
And apply them
And see what happens.

All strain and stress and tension will disappear
You will be at perfect peace.
Be at perfect peace now
And let Me use you.

God's Relationship With Us

I was aware of a strange throbbing in the atmosphere. It was rather like the beat of a heart.

I heard the words: 'It is the beat of the universal heart. Get into rhythm with it and become one with all life.'

Take time to be still
And listen to all the wonderful sounds around you
Enjoy them to the full
And give constant thanks
That you have ears to hear with.

How many times during the day do you stop
And listen to those many inner and outer sounds?
Do you ever stand still listening
Counting how many different sounds you
    can hear?

This will make you more sensitive
More alert
More aware.

When you have tried that
And become more and more aware of life
Everywhere around you
Why not try listening to those inner
    intangible sounds
Which can only be heard in absolute stillness -
That stillness which passes understanding
When you become in tune with the things of
    the spirit
With the things that really matter in life.

Deep joy can be experienced
In quiet prayer;
Great joy can be expressed
In a song
In the spoken word.

Your whole being can dance with joy
A smile speaks of joy
Strangers can share joy
Even when their language is not understood.

Joy is limited to no age group
The child
The youth
The mature
All share joy.

Joy is important to your spiritual well-being
And you need to express joy.

Give constant thanks
For the sheer joy of life and living
The joy of companionship with each other
The joy of being attuned
To all the joyous things in life.
I AM JOY.

There are many paths
But the goal is the same in each.

There is always the easy way
Or the hard way of reaching the goal.

There is the direct route
Or the devious route
Which leads up highways and byways.
The choice is always up to the individual.

You are absolutely free
To choose your own path.
Therefore seek and follow it
And in the end you will reach the goal:
Your self-realisation of Me
The divinity within you.

My limitless love
My limitless truth
My limitless wisdom
Has no beginning and no ending
But is from everlasting to everlasting.

Awaken to this fact
Accept it
Absorb it
Until it becomes a part of you.

It is life
Life more abundant.

The very heavens are yours
For all I have is yours
And you are Mine
We are one now and forever.
Give eternal thanks for everything.

I am that I am

My life fills your being
My light fills your mind
My love fills your heart.

All is one
All is whole

Feel My life flowing
Vibrating throughout your whole being
Renewing, restoring, making whole.

As My light fills your mind
Be aware of the clarity of vision
Freeing you from all doubt and confusion
Dispelling all darkness.

As My love fills your heart
Love flows through you
Out to all you come in contact with.

All is one
All is whole.

Your mind, body and spirit are quickened anew
As you are aware of My presence within you.

I am your source
The source of all life, all creation.
I am light
I am love
I am within you.

My divine law of wholeness is working in you
Freeing you of all negativity
Overcoming all obstacles, all challenges
Filling you with life, with energy
Renewing and strengthening you.

I am wisdom
I am guiding and directing your every action.
Keep constantly aware of Me, your divinity.

I am your all in all
I give you the keys to My storehouses
Of all good in the universe
All I have is yours.

My riches are beyond measure
They are limitless
I am the source of all your prosperity
Your cup of life is overflowing.

Be ever aware of My limitless abundance
And draw it to you
Rise above all sense of lack
Allow nothing to cause you anxiety.

Be absolutely free and at one with Me
Accept Me as the source of all your good.
Come to Me with open hearts and minds
So that I can fill you
With peace, love and limitless abundance.

Give eternal thanks for everything
Walk in My ways all the days of your life
Do My will.
Peace.

You can be revitalised, renewed and restored
By the powerful energies of life
That flow through you from the top of your head
To the soles of your feet.

Be consciously aware of your oneness
With the Source of all life
All creation
With Me.

Give eternal thanks
For the wonder of the realisation of oneness.
Go forth this day
In joy and wholeness.

Be renewed, refreshed and restored
Through your oneness with Me.

As you dwell upon this wondrous oneness with Me
You will find all those little worries
And anxious thoughts
Will fade from your mind.

Know that I am within
The unlimited creative power
That shapes the universe
And guides the stars.

Face every challenge fearlessly
In the full knowledge that there is only one power
And every obstacle will vanish into nothingness.

Accepting your oneness with Me the Beloved
Be filled with new zest this day.

Be aware of My energy-giving love
Surging through every cell of your body
Every corner of your mind
Making all things new
Restoring harmony and peace.

Give eternal thanks for everything
And know how mightily blessed you are.

I am with you
Whether you ascend to the heights
Or sink to the depths
I am there.

I am with you in the silence
When all is peace and harmony
Yet I am there when you call upon Me
When you are in trouble
And all is chaos and confusion around you.

I am closer than breathing
Nearer than hands and feet.

I am within you
Within all creation
All is one life
I am life
I am all in all.

Rejoice
Give eternal thanks
For we are one.

You are centred in My peace
That peace that nothing can disturb.

Although from time to time
You may encounter circumstances that disturb you
Or make you feel insecure or fearful
Become centred in Me
My presence within
And find tranquillity and peace.

I am within you
I am that still clear centre of perfect peace.

Be consciously aware of Me at all times
See me in everyone and everything.

I am there
See with eyes that really see
Hear with ears that really hear
And give constant thanks for everything.

No matter what is wrong
No matter what problems confront you
Or how things may seem
Trust in Me
In My presence and power.

Know that I am ever with you
Ready to guide and protect you.

Know and accept your oneness with Me.
Just knowing this
And being willing to accept this
Brings great happiness and joy.

Happiness comes from within yourself
Trust that divinity within
Walk and talk with Me, God within
Learn to listen to that still small voice
Deep within

In unity and oneness you can do all things
Be consciously aware of this
And go forward in faith.

Wherever you are, there I am
For I am in the very midst of you.

You are safe, secure and unafraid
When you are constantly aware of this.

When you step out into the unknown
Into strange unfamiliar places and situations
You are never alone
I am there guiding and directing you
Making the crooked places straight
And the rough places smooth.

My love is ever there
Surrounding and enfolding you
So go on your way rejoicing
With your hearts overflowing with love
    and gratitude.

Be at perfect peace
And know I am that I am
I am within all creation
I am within you.

Your being is aware of the travail
The Earth is going through.

Your being is going through this travail
You cannot separate yourself from it
There is no separation.

Let the healing balm of love flow through you
God is love
God is in each one of us.

We are whole
The Earth is whole
We blend with the wholeness of all creation.
I am that I am
Our life is one with God.

We are one
We are one
We are one

Our hearts beat to the rhythm of oneness
We are in tune with all life
We are in tune with the Infinite.

Behold the wonder of nature
And give eternal thanks for it.

In nature you see Me:
In the growth of a tree
In the colour of a flower
In the scent of a rose.

I am in everything
Be ever aware of this.

In the beauty and shape of a stone
In a tiny grain of sand
In the majesty of the mountains
I am there.

Flow with the rhythm of nature
Blend with all there is around you.

Become consciously aware of Me
And of My divine presence.

Invite Me to share your all with you
Take time to walk and talk with Me
And to listen to My still small voice.

Come closer
Ever closer
Feel that oneness
The wonder of being at perfect peace
Deep within
Because you are aware of your oneness with Me.

Love

I was shown a big shell rather like a clam. I watched it opening up very slowly. I noticed that every time anything came near, it closed down very quickly, and that each time this took place it had more and more difficulty in keeping open.

I heard the words: 'Keep your heart wide open, so the love can flow in and through you all the time, bringing more and more love into the world.'

My love is everywhere present
There is nowhere My love is not.

My love is at the very centre of your being
And radiates out to all with whom you
    come in contact.

My love is the very essence of every person.

If you find yourself in an inharmonious situation
I am there
Harmonising your thoughts and the
thoughts of others.

When you are faced with indecision
I am with you
Guiding and directing you
I will make the way plain.

When thoughts of fear and depression
    sweep over you
Know that I am with you
Protecting and stilling you
All fear will disappear
And peace will infil you.

My love is with you always
Be secure in it
And go forward in calmness and confidence
Knowing that My love is continuously working
In and through you.

Open yourself
To the inflow of divine love
Universal love.

Open the door of your heart
And allow nothing to stop that flow.
Keep that door open wide
So love and light can flow freely in
    and through you
And the life force is ever evident within you.

Love is the key
Love opens all doors
Why not use the key
Turn it
And see what happens.

It will open up a new life for you
A life filled with joy and happiness
For when love is flowing from you
Into the lives of those around you
It brings transformation
For love draws forth love.

Rest in My love
And feel its healing power
Feel it flowing freely through every cell
   of your body
Bringing wholeness, oneness.

As you become aware of that oneness
Everything in your life falls into place
In true perfection.

Trust in My love
Express that divine love to all you come
   in contact with.
As you give so do you receive.

Recognise that I am within
And do My will
Feel absolutely secure in My divine love
And radiate joy, love, happiness and freedom.

Be what I am
Live My life.

I am love
I am life
I am oneness
I am perfection in all things.

The more love you radiate out into the world
The more love will be returned to you.

Love can change your whole outlook on life
Love can even change the appearance of a person
Even the plainest person becomes beautiful
When the heart is filled with love.

Love does indeed transform and transmute
As nothing else can
Because it is the greatest power
The most uniting power in the universe.

It is love that will weld you together
Love that will make you one
Love that will enable you to see the best in others
Love that will surmount all difficulties
And all that would divide and separate you.

Love one another
I can tell you to love one another
But you have to do it.

You love
When you reach out to one another
And try to understand what makes each other tick.

Love breaks down all barriers
Maintains an even flow of love between you all
Without any ups and downs
Likes and dislikes.

Love should never be turned on and off like a tap.
When you love
Love wholeheartedly
Never be afraid to show your love.

You cannot hide love
It is there for all to see
All to share in.

Let that divine love within you flow freely
Love draws forth love
Keep your heart open
And love, love, love.

Relax
Release all stress, all tension
Rest in My love

Be still, calm and quiet in My love
Then pour it forth
Love
Love
And more love
To everyone and everything.

All need love
My divine love.

Be My channel
And be it now.

Love Me
And put Me first in everything.

You cannot know Me
And walk in My ways
And do My will
If you do not love Me

And you cannot love Me
Unless you love one another.

Many souls talk about their love for Me
Yet they do not know what it means
    to love themselves
To love their fellow humans.

The key is always love
You must learn to love what you are doing
To love those you are with
Love where you live
Love your surroundings
Love the very air you breathe
The very ground you walk upon.

Love everything you set your eyes upon
Love all
Be aware of your oneness with all creation.

I am in everything
In everyone
I am that I am
We are one.

Radiate love
Love
And more love.

As love is released into the world
A wonderful healing takes place
It is like balm poured into a wound
Healing and making whole.

Love starts within the individual
It starts within each one of you
And grows like a seed
Bursting forth
Revealing great beauty and wholeness.

This is what is taking place now
Be consciously aware of it all the time
And let nothing within you hold it up.

Never fail to give thanks
That you can be used in this way.

Release
Relax
Let Me use you
Now.

Divine love never changes
Is not affected by conditions
Situations
Or circumstances.

It never blows hot and cold
But is the same
Yesterday, today and forever.

It is useless talking about love
It has to be lived
Demonstrated
Expressed in life and living.

Love without action is dead.
Divine love knows no discrimination
No separation
But is all inclusive
And envelops everyone
This is divine love
Agapé.

When you really fill your days
With love and appreciation
You will know the true meaning of life

For life is love
And love is life
And I am love and life
All in one.

Love is unity and wholeness.

When you truly love
You are whole
You are one with all life.

My love for you is from everlasting to everlasting
Rise above all self-criticism
All self-condemnation
And know that you are made in My image
   and likeness
And see that perfection within.

Simply be what I am
Live My life
Knowing that I am within you
You are secure in My love.

My love flows through you as a vitalising force
And brings out the best in you
Revealing all your gifts and talents
Making your faith strong and unshakable
Revealing your wholeness.

When you are perfectly attuned to Me
You know what true freedom is
And you are filled with joy and happiness.

Then you can see Me in all your fellow humans
That divine spark that is within all.

See with eyes that see
Hear with ears that hear
And give eternal thanks.

My love is infinite
My love never fails
I will never fail you or forsake you.

Call upon Me at any time
I am there
I am within you
With Me all things are possible.

Listen to My still small voice within
And obey it
And all will be made clear
All doubt and fear dissolve
Divine order is established in your life and affairs.

It is more blessed to give than to receive
Therefore give
And give
And go on giving
And never count the cost.

As you learn to give
Without a thought for self
Or what you are going to get out of it
It will be returned to you a thousandfold.
This is the law.

Life is a two-way thing
A constant giving and receiving.

The Process

I saw a potter moulding what looked like a chalice. I saw him mould and remould it until he was satisfied with the size and shape. Then I saw him put it through all its various processes, but when it seemed to be complete it had either a crack or a flaw of some sort and it had to be cast out.

Then with infinite patience he started again until he was completely satisfied with what he was making.

I heard the words: 'Once I have laid My hand upon you, I will never let you go until I have completed My handiwork. Be at perfect peace.'

Ponder on the words 'Now is the time'
See the secret of a joyous, harmonious,
    satisfying life
As you accept that *now* is the only time.

Now is the only time there is.
No longer dwell on the past
Nor look for some future good.

Awake to the glorious *now*
Which is filled with all the goodness of God
Accept it all.

Accept the truth
That understanding is ours now
Healing is ours now
Abundant limitless supply is ours now
Harmony is ours now
Protection is ours now
Peace is ours now
Joy is ours now.

Joyously and gratefully
Accept that all is a gift
Live in harmony, joy and satisfaction *now*
We are at peace with ourselves
And with the world *now*.

Raise your consciousness
And realise that you are ageless
You are as young as time
As old as eternity.

As you live fully and gloriously
In the ever present now
You are always as young as the present.

You are constantly being reborn
In spirit and in truth
You cannot remain static in this spiritual life.

There is always something new and exciting
To learn and to do
Living in a state of expectancy
Keeps you ever alert and young.

It is when the mind becomes old and dull
Life loses all its sparkle and zest
Keep your mind alert
And you can never grow old.

The fountain of youth is in your consciousness
The joy of living is the elixir of life.

Peace
Serenity
Tranquillity is within you
Look not without for it.

Now is the time to find it
Not tomorrow
Or when everything is flowing smoothly.

No matter what is going on all around you
You can affirm and embody
That perfect peace, serenity and tranquillity
And by doing this
You can really help every situation
You can see all that is taking place
   in true perspective
Nothing and no one is warped or twisted.

Replace all negative thoughts
With loving positive ones
And go on your way rejoicing
I am with you.

Fill your heart and mind
With peace
Love
Serenity
Tranquillity.

Do this last thing at night before you go to sleep
Then first thing in the morning on wakening.

As you learn to do this
You will carry this wonderful state
    of consciousness
Into your everyday life and living.

Anything that has to be done really well
Needs practice
Be willing to practise
And go on practising
How to live a life of peace and serenity
Until you have mastered it
And it is part of you.

Start doing it now.

See your whole being filled with light
With new life.

See every cell vibrating with energy and vitality
See yourself whole
Be aware of the wholeness of all life.

See everything functioning in perfect rhythm
And harmony
The whole of the universe functions
    under divine law.

Be consciously aware
That you are part of that divine law
That you are part of that perfect rhythm.

Flow with it
Blend with it
Be it
Be it now.

Think wholeness
Be wholeness
Manifest wholeness in your lives and living.

To be a whole being
You need to know yourself
Know who you are
Know where you are going
Know what you are doing
Then go ahead in confidence
And live a whole, glorious and full life.

Never have any doubts about yourself
And about your ability to be whole.
As you think
So do you bring about.
Bring about only the very very best -
Unity
Oneness
Wholeness
Love.

Flow, flow with all that is going on
Flow with life
Let there be no strain, no resistance.

You are like a flower in the garden of life
Simply allow yourself to unfold
Very naturally and gently
And reveal the full beauty and wonder
That is there within you.

As you allow your true self to be revealed
You help to raise the vibrations all around you.

As each individual allows the Christ within
To be reflected without
Transformation comes about.

Let your self be transformed
And give eternal thanks that it is so.

Gently, easily our good flows to us
Just as a stream flows gently along its path.

The stream does not seem hurried
Or anxious about its eventual destination -
A river, a lake or an ocean.

Sometimes we allow ourselves to forget
That God is the source of our supply.
As we relax and flow
As a stream flows gently along with life
We find we are not anxious about our goals
Because we realise that God will supply our
    every need.

As a stream flows along
Various tributaries feed into it
As well as many rain showers
Thus keeping it full.

So it is with us
God is continually providing us with wisdom
To find new channels for greater good in our lives.

Today I give thanks that I am gently, easily
Flowing along with life
And my good comes to me
In overflowing measure.

The emptier you are
The easier it is for Me to fill you
With Myself
My love
My light
My life
Until your whole being is overflowing with Me
And you begin to understand
The meaning of our oneness.

Then I can really work in and through you
To bring about My wonders and glories.

As long as you are complacent and self-satisfied
Or full of self-concern, self-pity and selfishness
You build a hard shell around you
And that which is within
Has the greatest difficulty in finding away out
And expressing itself.

Keep your mind stayed on Me
And express Me in all that you do, say and think.

Flow into the new
In perfect joy, harmony and freedom.

Live by the spirit and by truth.
Allow Me to work in and through you
All the time.

Obey My still small voice
Without hesitation
Move freely and joyously doing My will
See all around you My wonders being manifested.

I am within you
It is what comes from the soul which matters
Everything stems
From that which is in the very centre
   of your being.

Like a stone thrown into the centre of a pond
The ripples go out from that centre
Out, out
And touch everything within its area.

'As a man thinketh so is he.'

Look for and see the very best in every situation
Never feel justified in feeling resentful or unhappy
Because of unfair or unjust treatment
For this does not contribute peace of mind
    or well-being.

Turn every negative thought and emotion
    into positive
Simply refuse to accept any negativity
Know that I am in everything and every situation
And keep your mind stayed on Me.

Know that I am the source of all -
All life
All well-being
And draw all from me
You will draw only the very best to you
Then never fail to give eternal thanks
    for everything.

Blessed is the person
Whose heart is overflowing with love and
thanksgiving
Who gives thanks for every good and perfect gift
Who recognises Me as the source
And the giver as My channel whom I work
   in and through.

The best way
To bring love and prosperity into your life
Is to bless everything
And give thanks for every increase which
   comes your way
And never take anything for granted
Or feel you have a right to it.

Recognise everything as a gift from Me
Give thanks and bless the food you eat
The roof over your head
Bless every member of this vast family
Which I have placed on your heart
And see Me in each one
See My love being expressed in and
through them.

Bless the work you do whatever it is
And bless those who work beside you and
    with you.

Let everything you do be done for the
    good of the whole
And to My honour and glory
And in love.

Action and Service

I was shown many, many people coming to live here in this centre of light - not just to live but to go out from here to work, infiltrating all the different places of work in a vast area, taking with them the spirit of the new age.

I could see this very clearly, and then the words came to me: 'See My light and love going out and across the whole world.'

When you breathe the breath of life
You breathe it in
But you cannot retain it for any length of time
Without breathing it out.

This is a two-way thing
Giving and receiving
Without it there would be no life.

Open your heart
And give all you can
Of the gifts which have been given to you.

Give of your love
Your wisdom
Your understanding.

Give of the intangible
As well as the tangible things
Which are yours.

Give wholeheartedly
And joyously
With no thought of the self.

You are My hands and feet
Therefore *you* have to take action.

One small guided action
Can open wide many firmly closed doors
Therefore be still
Take time to listen
So you do not fail to hear My instructions
Then act immediately.

Your relationship with any soul
Can be put right.
Keep the love flowing
And watch your reaction
Should the response not be immediate.

Love will always find a way.
Be very patient
Very loving.

Be My channel
And listen to My still small voice within.

As you obey My voice
You will know exactly what to do
Where to go
How to do what has to be done.

In peace and stillness
Be aware of My divine presence
And know I am in the midst of you
And all is very very well.

Peace be with you.

Faith without works is empty.
Live and demonstrate your faith
So that all may see what it really means to you
And how it grows stronger
As you put it into practice
In small ways to begin with
Then gradually in every area of your living.

When a small child starts to walk
It takes a few faltering steps
Until it gains confidence.

As it does so
Its steps become firmer and surer
Until eventually it can walk without stumbling.

Then it learns to run and jump
But one stage has to be reached at a time.

So with faith
It has to be built up gradually
It does not come all at once
Be patient
And keep on keeping on.

One can never know what is possible until
  one tries
The most important part of any project
Is the decision to go ahead.

I choose to go ahead
With whatever now needs to be done in my life
I have faith.

I know nothing is impossible
When the Beloved is guiding and directing me
He knows what is best for me.

In the stillness
I feel my oneness with the Beloved
All that I need is being given to me
Strength
Understanding
Wisdom
Love in limitless abundance.

I lift up my heart
In deep gratitude for everything
Having made my decision to go ahead in faith
I know I will succeed.

The Beloved is ever with me
Ever within me.

Serve Me through your daily work
In everything you do, say and think.

Serve Me in the little things
And big things in your daily lives.

Do not leave Me out of anything
And never divide your life into compartments
But realise it is all one life
And live it to the full in this way.

I tell you many times to live a life
Not just talk about it.

There is far too much talk
And not enough action in the world today
Which is why the world is in the state it is in.

You are the ones to live that life
To put into action what I am telling you
You have to do the work
No one else can do it for you.

You can be given a glass of water
But you have to do the drinking
You can be given a plate of food
But only you can eat it
If you are to be nourished by it.

You can be told spiritual truths
But only as you live them
Put them into practice
Demonstrate them in your life
Do they become reality to you
And live and move and have their being in you.

You must do your own work
Your own thinking
Your own living
Your own working things out
You must stand on your own feet
And never expect anyone else to do it for you.

Enjoy every moment of living
For the joy of the Beloved fills our souls
And blesses us with the appreciation of
   the gift of life itself.

Find joy in the work you do
In the times of peace and leisure
In the times we spend together.

Joy fills us with strength
And enables us to do what needs to be done
With enthusiasm and optimism.

Joy looks beyond appearances
To the best in every experience
And in every outcome.

Joy unites us with the Beloved within
  each one of us
Joy opens our hearts
So we are aware of the Christ within
Joy inspires us
To give the best we can give to life at all times
Joy keeps us steadfast in faith.

Joy helps us to see the light
At the end of the dark tunnel of human challenges
And rekindles in us
The will and the desire to begin again.

The fruit of the Spirit is joy
So let there be more joy in your life
More fun and laughter.

It is so important
That there is balance in all things
So that life can be enjoyed to the full.

For when there is joy and happiness
You are aware of Me
And My divine presence.

Faith without works is dead.

Life without love
Is like a desert without water
Dry
Parched
Incapable of bringing forth a living thing.

Therefore keep your heart open
And the love flowing
No matter what is happening around you.

Live a vital living life
Bringing forth life
And more life.

You cannot prove anything
Unless you put it to the test
You have to step out in faith
And do the seemingly impossible.

You have to learn to live beyond yourself
Beyond your limits
To prove that with Me all things are possible.

To live within your own small self
Afraid to reach out beyond your limits
Afraid to put life to the test
Will get you nowhere
You will fail to see My hand in everything.

Fear nothing
Know that I am with you always
I will guide and direct your every step.

Expect miracle upon miracle
And see them come about
See the new heaven and new Earth manifest
As you learn to live this life
And make it work.

I *am love*
I am light
I am peace
I am limitless abundance

Know that wherever I am, you are
For we are one
For deep within your heart is
Love
Light
Peace
Abundance.

Dwell on these words
Love
Light
Peace
Abundance
Until you know that you embody them
That they are a part of you
And all that is not of the highest is transmuted.

You can transcend all negativity
When you realise that the only power it has
   over you
Is your belief in it.

As you experience this truth about yourself
You are set free.

Give constant thanks for the awareness of the truth
And walk in it.

Go into the silence
Feel peace and serenity steal over you
And enfold you.

In that state of perfect peace
Ask and receive My blessings.

Then go forward
In absolute faith and confidence
Do what has to be done
Know that I am with you all the way
That everything will work out perfectly.

The greater the task to be accomplished
The greater the faith and need of My blessing.

Learn to bring Me into every area of your life
So all is blessed by Me.

For am I not within each one of you?
Be consciously aware of this at all times.

Go forward and upward
Always reaching for the highest.

Life is movement
It is change
It is growth.

No soul can remain in the same state
   all the time
Nature cannot remain static
It is ever changing and expanding
Growing from one stage to the next.

The acorn grows to a mighty oak
The bulb grows and produces beautiful flowers
The seed of corn produces wheat.

Change is taking place all the time
Do not resist change
But flow with it
Accept it.

It may not always be comfortable
Be willing to accept a little discomfort
So that the glorious new can evolve
   in and through you
Transforming you into a new being
Filled with light
Love
And inspiration.

Be willing to move forward into the unknown
Without fear or trepidation
To pioneer something entirely new.
There will be no well-worn ruts to go along
But vast new areas to explore
And it will be tremendously exciting.

Let Me guide each one of you
Every step along the way
And the whole plan will unfold in true perfection.

One door after another will be flung wide open
Nothing will be allowed to stand in the way
Many different aspects of the work will open up
And will develop at the same time
Many different aspects of the plan will unfold
And you will each have your part to play in it.

Put Me first in everything
Then nothing can go wrong.
These are thrilling times you are living in
And anything can happen
At any moment.

Expect miracle upon miracle
See them come about
And give Me eternal thanks.

I was shown what looked like a volcano erupting. The lava was flowing down all sides and seemed to be spreading everywhere.
I heard the words:

'Let your lives erupt in sheer joy
And let the love flow forth freely
To everyone and everything
Transforming all.'

Other works by Eileen Caddy
(published by Findhorn Press)

books

Opening Doors Within

Waves of Spirit

Choosing to Love

God Spoke to Me

The Dawn of Change

Footprints on the Path

Foundations of a Spiritual Community

The Spirit of Findhorn

audio-tapes

Be Still: Meditation for the Child Within

Why Meditate?

Loving Unconditionally

Faith and the Power of Prayer

The Challenge of Change

For a complete catalogue of Findhorn Press books and products, please fill in this form and send it to:

Findhorn Press
The Press Building
The Park, Findhorn
Forres IV36 0TZ
Scotland
fax 01309 690036

or

Findhorn Press
P. O. Box 13939
Tallahassee
Florida 32317-3939
USA

or email your request to

books@findhorn.org